THE WAR IN THE MOUNTAINS

THE WAR IN
THE MOUNTAINS

by

Rudyard Kipling

UNIFORM
PRESS

Uniform Press Ltd
66 Charlotte Street
London
W1T 4QE

www.uniformpress.co.uk

First published in 1917
This edition published in 2015 by Uniform Press Ltd

978-1-910500-149

5 4 3 2 1

Printed in India by Imprint Digital
Designed by Charlotte Glyde

CONTENTS

I

THE ROADS OF AN ARMY
JUNE 6TH 1917

WHEN one reached the great Venetian plain near Army Headquarters, the Italian fronts were explained with a clearness that made maps unnecessary.

'We have three fronts,' said my informant. 'On the first, the Isonzo front, which is the road to Trieste, our troops can walk, though the walking is not good. On the second, the Trentino, to the north, where the enemy comes nearest to our plains, our troops must climb and mountaineer, you will see.'

He pointed south-east and east across the heat haze to some evil-looking ridges a long way off where there was a sound of guns debating ponderously. 'That is the Carso, where we are going now,' he said; then he turned north-east and north where nearer, higher mountains showed streaks of snow in their wrinkles.

'Those are the Julian Alps,' he went on. 'Tolmino is behind

7

them, north again. Where the snow is thicker – do you see? – are the Carnic Alps; we fight among them. Then to the west of them come the Dolomites, where tourists used to climb and write books. There we fight, also. The Dolomites join on to the Trentino and the Asiago Plateau, and there we fight. And from there we go round north till we meet the Swiss border. All mountains, you see?'

He picked up the peaks one after another with the ease of a man accustomed to picking up landmarks at any angle and any change of light. A stranger's eyes could make out nothing except one sheer rampart of brooding mountains – 'like giants at a hunting' all along the northern horizon.

The glass split them into tangled cross-chains of worsted hillocks, hollow-flanked peaks cleft by black or grey ravines, stretches of no-coloured rock gashed and nicked with white, savage thumbnails of hard snow thrust up above cockscombs of splinters, and behind everything an agony of tortured crags against the farthest sky. Men must be borne or broke to the mountains to accept them easily. They are too full of their own personal devils.

The plains around Udine are better – the fat, flat plains crowded with crops – wheat and barley patches between trim vineyards, every vine with her best foot forwards and arms spread to welcome spring. Every field hedged with old, strictly pollarded mulberry-trees for the silkworms, and every road flanked with flashing water-channels that talk pleasantly in the heart.

At each few score yards of road there was a neat square

of limestone road-metal, with the water-channel led squarely round it. Each few hundred yards, an old man and a young boy worked together, the one with a long spade, the other with a tin pot at the end of a pole. The instant that any wear showed in the surface, the elder padded the hollow with a spoonful of metal, the youth sluiced it, and at once it was ready to bind down beneath the traffic as tight as an inner-tube patch.

There was curiously little traffic by our standards, but all there was moved very swiftly. The perfectly made and tended roads do most of the motor's work. Where there are no bumps there can be no strain, even under maximum loads. The lorries glide from railhead to their destination, return, and are off again without overhaul or delay. On the simple principle that transportation is civilisation, the entire Italian campaign is built, and every stretch of every road proves it.

But on the French front Providence does not supply accommodating river-beds whence the beautiful self-binding stuff can be shovelled ready-made into little narrow-gauge trucks all over the landscape. Nor have we in France solid mountains where man has but to reach out his hand to all the stone of all the pyramids. Neither, anywhere, have we populations expert from birth at masonry. To parody Macaulay, what the axe is to the Canadian, what the bamboo is to the Malay, what the snow-block is to the Esqimaux, stone and cement is to the Italian, as I hope to show later.

They are a hard people habituated to handling hard stuffs, and, I should imagine, with a sense of property as keen as the Frenchman's. The innumerable grey-green troops in the bright fields moved sympathetically among the crops and did not litter their surroundings with rubbish. They have their own pattern of steel helmet, which differs a little from ours, and gives them at a distance a look of Roman Legionaires on a frieze of triumph. The infantry and, to a lesser extent, other arms are not recruited locally but generally, so that the men from all parts come to know each other, and losses are more evenly spread. But the size, physique, and, above all, the poise of the men struck one at every step. They seem more supple in their collective movements and less loaded down with haberdashery than either French or British troops. But the indescribable difference lay in their tread – the very fall of their feet and the manner in which they seemed to possess the ground they covered. Men whose life runs normally in the open, own and are owned by their surroundings more naturally than those whom climate and trade keep housed through most of the year. Space, sunlight, and air, the procession of life under vivid skies, furnish the Italian with a great deal of his mental background, so when, as a soldier, he is bidden to sit down in the clean dust and be still as the hours while the shells pass, he does so as naturally as an Englishman draws a chair to the fire.

The Belly of Stones

'And that is the Isonzo River,' said the officer, when we reached the edge of the Udine plain. It might have come out from Kashmir with its broad sweeps of pale shoals that tailed off downstream into dancing haze. The milky jade waters smelt of snow from the hills as they plucked at the pontoon bridges' moorings which were made to allow for many feet rise and fall. A snow-fed river is as untrustworthy as a drunkard.

The flavour of mules, burning fuels, and a procession of high-wheeled Sicilian carts, their panels painted with Biblical stories, added to the Eastern illusion. But the ridge on the far side of the river that looked so steep, and was in reality only a small flattish mound among mountains, resembled no land on earth. If the Matoppos had married the Karroo they might have begotten some such abortion of stone-speckled, weather-hacked dirt. All along the base of it, indifferent to the thousands of troops around, to the scream of mules, the cough of motors, the whirr of machinery and the jarring carts, lay in endless belts of cemeteries those Italian dead who had first made possible the way to the heights above.

'We brought them down and buried them after each fight,' said the officer. 'There were many fights. Whole regiments lie there – and there – and there. Some of them died in the early days when we made war without roads, some of them died afterwards, when we had the roads but the Austrians had the guns. Some of them died at the last when we beat the Austrians. Look!'

As the poet says, the battle is won by the men who fall. God knows how many mothers' sons sleep along the river before Gradisca in the shadow of the first ridge of the wicked Carso. They can hear their own indomitable people always blasting their way towards the east and Trieste. The valley of the Isonzo multiplies the roar of the heavy pieces around Goritzia and in the mountains to the north, and sometimes enemy aeroplanes scar and rip up their resting-places. They lie, as it were, in a giant smithy where the links of the new Italy are being welded under smoke and flame and heat – heat from the dry shoals of the river-bed before, and heat from the dry ridge behind them.

The road wrenched itself uphill among the dead trenches, through wire entanglements red-rusted on the ground – looking like 'harrows fit to reel men's bodies out like silk' – between the usual mounds of ruptured sand-bags, and round empty gun-pits softened at their angles by the passage of the seasons.

Trenches cannot be dug, any more than water can be found, on the Carso, for a spade's depth below the surface the unkindly stone turns to sullen rock, and everything must be drilled and blasted out. For the moment, because spring had been wet, the stones were greened over with false growth of weeds which wither utterly in the summer, leaving the rocks to glare and burn alone. As if all this savagery were not enough, the raw slopes and cusps of desolation were studded with numberless pits and water-sinks, some exquisitely designed by the Devil for machine-gun positions, others like small craters capable of holding eleven-inch howitzers, which opened at the bottom through rifts into dry caverns where regiments can hide – and be dug out.

We wound under the highest rise of the ridge and came out on its safest side, on to what the Arabs would call a belly of stones. There was no pretence of green – nothing but rock, broken and rebroken, as far as the eye could carry, by shell-fire, as though it were the far end of Lydd ranges. Earth, however battered, one can make some sort of shift to walk on, but here there was no more foothold than in a nightmare. No two splinters were the same size, and when a man stumbled on the edge of a shell-crater, its sides rolled down with the rattle of a dried tongue in the mouth. Great communal graves were heaped up and walled down their long sides with stone, and on one such stack of death's harvest some one had laid an old brown thigh-bone. The place shivered with ghosts in the hot daylight as the stones shivered in the heat. Dry, ragged points, like a cow's hips, rose along the ridge which we had overlooked. One of them only a few feet lower than where we stood had been taken and lost six times. 'They cleared us out with machine-guns from where we are now,' said the officer, 'so we had to capture this higher point first. It cost a good deal.'

He told us tales of regiments wiped out, reconstituted and wiped out anew, who achieved, at their third or fourth resurrection, what their ancestors had set out to win. He told us of enemy dead in multitudes put away somewhere beneath the ringing stones, and of a certain Austrian Honvéd division which by right of blood claim that this section of the Carso is specially theirs to defend. They, too, appear out of the rocks, perish, and are born again to be slain.

'If you come into this shell-hole – I don't think I should stand up too much – I'll try to show you what we want to do at our next push,' the officer said. 'We're just getting ready for it' – and he explained with a keen forefinger how it was intended to work along certain hills that dominate certain roads which lead, at last, towards the head of the Adriatic – one could see it, a patch of dull silver to the southward – under some dark, shadowy hills that covered Trieste itself.

A sun-warmed water-pipe crossed our shell-hole at about the height of one's chin, and the whirr of a distant shell. The officer's explanation was punctuated by the grumble of single big guns on the Italian side, ranging in anticipation of the serious work to come. Then the ground hiccupped a few yards in front of us, and stones – the poisonous edged stones of the Carso – whirred like partridges. 'Mines,' said the officer serenely, while the civils automatically turned up their collars. 'They are working up the steep side of the ridge, but they might have warned us!'

The mines exploded in orderly line, and it being impossible to run away over the stones, one had to watch them with the lively consciousness that those scores of thousands of dead beneath and around and behind were watching too. A pneumatic drill chattered underground, as teeth chatter.

'I didn't know there were so many loose stones in the world,' I said.

'They are not all loose. We wish they were. They're very solid. Come and see!'

Out of the grinning sunshine we walked into a great rock-cut gallery with rails running underfoot and men shovelling rubbish into trucks. Half-a-dozen embrasures gave light through thirty feet of rock. 'These are some of the new gun-positions,' said the officer. 'For six-inch guns perhaps! Perhaps for eleven.'

'And how'd you get eleven-inch guns up here?' I asked.

He smiled a little – I learned the meaning of that smile up in the mountains later.

'By hand,' said he, and turned to the engineer in charge to reprove him for exploding the mines without warning.

We came off the belly of stones, and when we were on the flat lands beyond the Isonzo again, looked back at it across its girdling line of cemeteries. It was the first obstacle Italy found at her own threshold, after she had forced the broad uneasy Isonzo, 'where troops can walk, though the walking is not good.' It seemed enough.

II

PODGORA

JUNE 9TH 1917

'WE have finished with stones for a little,' said the officer. 'We are going to a mountain of mud. It is dry now, but this winter it never stayed quiet.'

An acre or so of the the climbing roadside was still uneasy, and had slid face-down in a splatter of earth and tree-roots which men were shovelling off.

'It's rather a fresh road. Altogether we have about four thousand miles of new roads – and old roads improved – on a front of about six hundred kilometres. But you see, our kilometres are not flat.'

The landscape, picked out in all the greens of spring, was that of early Italian holy pictures – the same isolated, scarred hummocks rising from enamelled meadows or drifts of bloom into the same elaborate entablatures of rock, crowned by a campanile or tufted with dark trees. On the white roads beneath

16

us the lines of motors and mule transport strung out evenly to their various dumps. At one time we must have commanded twenty full miles, all working at once, but never could we spy a breakdown. The Italian transport system has been tried out by war long ago.

The more the road sunk to the plains, the more one realised the height of the mountains dominating us all round. Podgora, the mountain of mud, is a little Gibraltar about eight hundred feet high, almost sheer on one side, overlooking the town of Gorizia, which, in civil life, used to be a sort of stuffy Cheltenham for retired Austrian officers. Anywhere else, Podgora hill might be noticeable, but you could set down half-a-dozen Gibraltars among this upheaval of hills, and in a month the smooth Italian roads would overrun them as vine tendrils overrun rubbish-heaps. The lords of the military situation round Gorizia are the four and five-thousand-foot mountains, crowded one behind the other, every angle, upland and valley of each offering or masking death.

The mountains are vile ground for aeroplane work, because there is nowhere to alight in comfort, but nonetheless the machines beat over them from both sides, and the anti-aircraft guns which are not impressive in the open plains fill the gorges with multiplied coughings more resembling a lion's roar than thunder. The enemy fly high, over the mountains, and show against the blue like bits of whirling ash off a bonfire. They drop their bombs generously, and the rest is with fate – either the blind crack on blank rock and the long harmless whirr of slivered stone, or that ripe crash which tells that timber, men and mules have caught it full this time. If all the setting were not so lovely, if the lights, the leafage, the blossom, and the butterflies mating on the grassy lips of old trenches were not allowed to insult the living workmen of death, their work would be easier to describe without digressions.

When we had climbed on foot up and up and into the bowels of the mountain of mud, through galleries and cross-galleries, to a discreetly veiled observation-point, Gorizia, pink, white, and bluish, lay, to all appearance, asleep beneath us amid her full flowering chestnut-trees by the talking Isonzo. She was in Italian hands – won after furious fights – but the enemy guns from the mountains could still shell her at pleasure, and the next move, said our officer, would be to clear certain heights – 'Can you see our trenches creeping up to them?' – from their menace. There and there, he pointed, the Italian troops would climb and crawl, while thus and thus would the fire of our guns cover them, till they came to that bare down and must make their rush – which is really a climb – alone. If that rush failed, then they must dig in among the rocks, and lie out under the bitter skyline, for this was war among the mountains where the valleys were death-traps and only heights counted.

Then we turned to the captured hills behind us that had lived so unconsidered since they were made, but now, because of the price paid for them, would stand forth memorable as long as Italy was remembered. The heathen mountains in front had yet to be baptized and entered on the roll of honour, and one could not say at that moment which one of them would be most honourable, or what cluster of herdsmen's huts would

18

carry the name of a month's battle through the ages.

The studied repose that heralds a big push cloaked both lines. No one, except a few pieces who were finishing some private work, was saying anything. The Austrians had their own last touches to put in too. They were ranging on a convent up a hillside – one deliberate shell at a time. A big gun beneath us came lazily into the game on our side, shaking the whole mountain of mud, and then asking questions of its observing officer across the valley.

Suddenly a boy's voice, that had been taking corrections, spoke quite unofficially at the receiver in the gloom under our feet. 'Oh! Congratulations!' it cried. 'Then you dine with us to-night, and you'll pay for the wine.'

Every one laughed.

'Rather a long walk,' said our guide and friend. 'The observing officer – he is down near Gorizia – has just telephoned that he has been promoted to Aspirant – Sub-Lieutenant, don't you say? He will have to climb up here to the artillery Mess tonight and stand drinks on his promotion.'

'I bet he'll come,' someone said. There were no takers. So you see, youth is always immortally the same.

Gorizia

We dropped from Podgora into Gorizia by a road a little more miraculous than any we had yet found. It was in the nature of a toboggan-run, but so perfectly banked at the corners that the traffic could have slid down by itself if it had been allowed.

As we entered the town, men were mending the bridge across the river – for a reason. They do a great deal of mending in Gorizia. Austrians use heavy pieces on the place – twelve-inch stuff sometimes – dealt methodically and slowly from far back, out of the high hills. I tried to find a house that did not carry that monotonous stippling of shrapnel, but it was difficult. The guns reach everywhere.

There was no air in the still hollow where the place lay – hardly a whisper among the domed horse-chestnuts. Troops were marching through to their trenches far up the hillside beyond, and the sound of their feet echoed between the high garden-walls where the service wires were looped among pendants of wisteria in full flower.

There are several hundred civilians in the city who have not yet cared to move, for the Italian is as stubborn in these things as the Frenchman. In the main square where the house-fronts are most battered and the big electric-light standard bows itself to the earth, I saw a girl bargaining for some buttons on a card at a shop-door – hands, eyes, and gesture, all extravagantly employed, and the seller as intently absorbed as she. It must be less distracting than one thinks to live under the knowledge one is always being watched from above – breathed upon in the nape of the neck, so to speak, by invisible mouths.

A little later I was being told confidentially by some English woman among a garden of irises, who owned a radiographic installation and a couple of shrapnel-dusted cars, that they had been promised, when the push came, that they and their apparatus might go into Gorizia itself, to a nice underground room, reasonably free from shells which disconcert the wounded and jar the radiograph, and 'wasn't it kind of the authorities?'

The Ridge of the Waiting Guns

The amazing motor-lorries were thicker on the more amazing road than they had been. Our companion apologised for them. 'You see, we have been taking a few things up to the Front in this way in the last few days,' he said.

'Are all Italians born driving motors?' I demanded, as a procession of high-hooded cars flopped down the curve we were breasting, pivoted on its outside edge, their bonnets pointing over a four-hundred-foot drop, and slid past us with a three-inch clearance between hub and hub.

'No,' he replied. 'But we, too, have been at the game a long time. I expect all the bad chauffeurs have been killed.'

'And bad mules?' One of them was having hysterics on what I thought – till I had climbed a few thousand higher – was the edge of a precipice. 'Oh, you can't kill a mule,' and sure enough, when the beast had registered its protest, it returned to the dignity of its sires. The muleteer said not a word.

We bored up and into the hills by roads not yet mapped, but solid as lavish labour can make them against the rolling load of the lorries, and the sharp hoofs of the mule, as well as the wear and tear of winter, who is the real enemy. Our route ran along the folded skirts of a range not more than three or four thousand feet high, more or less parallel with the Isonzo in its way from the north. Rivers that had roared level beside us dropped and shrunk to blue threads half visible through the forest. Mountains put forward hard shaly knees round which we climbed in a thousand loops that confused every sense of direction. Then, because the enemy seven miles off, could see, stretches of the crowded road were blinded with reed mats while torn holes above or below us proved that he had searched closely.

After that, the colossal lap of a mountain alive with dripping waters would hide us in greenery and moisture, till the sight of a cautious ash-tree still in bud – her sister ten minutes ago had been clothed from head to foot – told us we had risen again to the heights of the naked ridge. And here were batteries upon batteries of the heaviest pieces, so variously disposed and hidden that finding one gave you no clue to the next. Elevens, eights, fours – sixes, and elevens again, on caterpillar wheels, on navy mountings adapted for land work, disconnected from their separate tractors, or balanced and buttressed on their own high speed motors, were repeated for mile after mile, with their ammunition caves, their shops, and the necessary barracks for their thousand servants studded or strung out on the steep drop behind them. Obscure pits and hollows hid them pointing to heaven, and how they had been brought up to be lowered there passed imagination as they peeped out of the merest slits in green sod. They stood back under ledges and eaves of the ground where no light could outline them, or became one with a dung-heap behind a stable. They stalled themselves in thick forest growth, like elephants at noon, or, as it were, crawled squat on their bellies to the very bows of crests overlooking seas of mountains, they, like the others down the line, were waiting for the hour and the order. Not half-a-dozen out of a multitude opened their lips.

When we had climbed to a place appointed, the shutter of an observation-post opened upon the world below. We saw the Isonzo almost vertically beneath us, and on the far side were the Italian trenches that painfully climbed to the crest of the bare ridges where the infantry live, who must be fed under cover of night until the Austrians are driven out of their heights above.

'It is just like fighting a burglar across housetops,' said the officer. 'You can spot him from a factory chimney, but he can spot you from the spire of the cathedral – and so on.'

'Who sees those men down yonder in the trenches?' I asked. 'Everybody on both sides, but our guns cover them. That is the way in our war. Height is everything.'

He said nothing of the terrific labour of it all, before a man or a gun can come into position – nothing of the battle that was fought in the gorge below when the Isonzo was crossed and the Italian trenches clawed and sawed their red way up the hillside, and very little of the blood-drenched snout of the height called the Sabotino that was carried, lost and recarried most gloriously in the old days of the War, and now lay out below as innocent-seeming as a mountain pasture.

They are a hard people, these Latins, who have had to fight the mountains and all that is in them, metre by metre, and are thankful when their battlefields do not slope at more than forty-five degrees.

III

A Pass, a King and a Mountain
June 13th 1917

A falcon swooped off the hill-top and hung below us
searching the valley at the head of the pass, which was
a broad grassy funnel dipping out into space, exactly like the
Muttianee behind Simla. The usual roughly paved caravan
track led over it between hummocks of board, rock, and earth,
whence it seemed only right that Hillmen would presently
come out with brick-tea. But it was a gunner with kindly offers
of coffee – a weather-worn commander whose eyes were set
to views of very distant horizons. He and his guns lived up
there all the year, and on the highest grazing-grounds on either
side of his lair were black shell-holes by the score, where the
enemy had hunted for him. The snow had just gone, neatly
turning in the winter-killed grass-stems around the edge of
the older shell-holes as it melted away. This Commandant,

like the others, controlled an observation post. When he clicked back its shutter, we looked down as the falcons do, into an Austrian town with a broken bridge over a river, and lines of Italian trenches, crawling towards it across river flats – all laid out mapwise, three thousand feet below. The town waits – as Gorizia waits – while decisions of which it knows nothing are being taken overhead, whether it shall live or die. Meanwhile, the Commandant pointed out its beauties, for it was his possession, you see, by right of eminent domain, and he dispensed the high, the low, and the middle justice over it.

When we were at coffee, a subaltern came with word that the Austrians, ten thousand metres away, were shifting something that looked like a gun. (Guns take all sorts of shapes when they have to be moved.) The Commandant excused himself, and the telephones called up observers laid out somewhere among the tangled steeps and hanging woods below.

'No,' he said presently, shaking his head, 'it's only a cart – not worth a shot just now.'

There was much bigger game afoot elsewhere, and I fancy that the orders were not to flush it too soon.

The keen wind whooped over the grass and drummed on the boards of the huts. A soldier at a bench fitted nails into his boot, and crooned to himself as he tapped. A blast or two exploded somewhere down the newly-made screened road along which we had come, and the echoes clamoured through the valley. Then a motor-horn with a distinctive note rang fierce and piercing.

'That's the King's bugle,' someone said. 'He may be coming here. Listen. No… he's going on to look at some of the new batteries. You never know where he'll turn up, but he's always somewhere along the line, and he never leaves anything unseen.'

The remark was not addressed to the private with the boot, but he grinned as men do at the name of a popular general. Many pleasant tales are current in his armies concerning the King of Italy. The gist of them all is that he is very much of a man as well as a statesman. Kings and ammunition-dumps are fair targets for aeroplanes, but, if the tale be true, and it squares with all the others, there is one King at least who shoots back and shoots straight. No fear or circumstance distinguish him from any other general in field kit, down to the single ribbon that testifies to a year's war service. He moves temperate, loyal, keen, in stark simplicity among his men and full hazards of war.

All that day a triangular snow peak had risen like a master wave, now to one side, now to the other, of our road. On the steepest slopes of its topmost snows it carried a broad, open 'V,' miles long on either limit, which appeared in the changing lights like a faint cattle-brand, or giant ski-tracks, or those dim canals of Schiaparelli which mark the face of the red planet Mars. That was Monte Nero, and the mark was the line of the Italian trenches on it. They are cut through snow that melts, into packed snow that never melts, into packed snow that never softens; and where the snow cannot lie on the sheer rocks, they are blasted in and out among the frost-ridden rubbish of the mountain crest. Up there, men fight with field-guns, machine-guns, and rifles, and more deadly shoots of stones heaped together and sent sliding down at the proper time. Up there, if a man is wounded and bleeds only a little before he is found, the cold kills him in minutes, not hours. Whole companies can be frostbitten and crippled even while they lie taking cover in the pauses of a rush, and the wandering mountain gusts take sentries from under the lee of their rock as they stand up to be relieved, and flick them into space.

The mountain draws its own supplies and troops for miles and miles back, over new roads that break off from the main arteries of traffic and split into mule-trails and man-tracks, emerging, at last, against the bare rocks, as thin and threadlike as the exposed roots of a botanical diagram to illustrate capillary attraction. There has never been a greater work of invention, preparation, and endurance among fantastic horrors than the winning and holding of this one post. And it has passed almost unnoticed by nations, each absorbed in its own hell.

'We climbed! We climbed! We carried the approaches. Now we are up there, and the Austrians are a little to the right just above that sinking cloud under that cliff. When they are dislodged we get full command of that height,' etc., etc. The officer spoke without emotion. He and a few million others had been goaded out of their known life to achieve the incredible. They had left the faculty of wonder at home with the pictures and the wallpapers and the unfit.

ARMIES AND AVALANCHES

'But if you make a road, you must make a road,' the officer insisted.

'Admitted. But can all these tremendous works be necessary?'

'Believe me, we do not lay one stone more than we have to. You are seeing the roads in spring. We make them for winter in the mountains. They must be roads to stand everything.'

They clung to the hillside on hanging arches of concrete, they were riveted and sheathed thirty or forty feet down with pointed masonry; protected above by stonewallings that grew out of the rock itself, and above that again, by wing walls to part and divert uneasy snow-slides or hopping stones a quarter of a mile uphill. They were pierced by solid bridges and culverts at every turn where drainage might gather, or flanked with long aprons of pitched stone, where some mountain's soaked side slid down in broad fans of stony trash which, when the snows melt, delivers sudden blasts of racing pebbles and water.

Every few hundred yards on the road were the faithful old man and the boy, the stone-heap and the spade, and the twenty-mile-an-hour lorries rolled as smoothly over the flawless surface as they had in the plains.

We passed a Touring Club notice, of peace times, bidding people 'pay attention' to avalanches. A tangle of pines, snapped like straws underneath one drunken boulder about the size of a house, underlining the warning.

'Yes, before the War, people used to whisper and hold their breath when they passed some of these corners in winter. And now! Hear what a noise that string of cars makes in these gorges! Imagine it in winter! Why, a single motor-bus sometimes would start an avalanche! We've lost many men that way. But transport can't stop for snow.'

It did not. We ran, as the lorries ran, into patches of melting snow, fringed with gentian clumps, heath, and crocus! These patches thickened to sheets, till at the head of a pass we found ten foot of packed snow, all newly shovelled back from the dry, perfectly graded road-bed. It trailed after us brokenly, through villages whose gutters danced with bright water, and closed up abreast of us in sheets once more when we reached Cortina.

This was an ex-health and pleasure resort, which of late belonged to the Austrians, who filled it with 'new-art' hotels, each more villainous in design than its neighbour. Today, as the troops and transport come and go, the jigsaw and coloured-glass atrocities look like bedizened ladies, standing distracted in the middle of a police raid. The enemy do not shell the hotels much, because they are owned by Austrian heyducs who hope to come back and resume their illustrious trade.

In the old days, whole novels were written about Cortina. The little-used mountains round made an impressive background for love-tales and climbing adventures. Love has gone out of this huge basin of the Dolomites now, and the mountaineering is done by platoons in order to kill men, not by individuals who read papers before Alpine Clubs.

On most of the other Fronts war is waged in hot contact with all man's work and possessions. The slayer and the slain keep each other company at least in a world that they themselves created. But here one faces the immense scorn of the hills preoccupied with their own affairs; for between frost, snow, and undermining waters, the hills are always busy. Men, mules, and motors are busy too! The roads are alive with them. They inhabit cities inside dim forests of pine whose service paths are cut through stale snow and whose aisles ring with machinery! They march out, marshal, and distribute themselves among the snowfields above, by whole regiments and arsenals at a time. Take your eye off them for an instant, and they are swallowed up in the vastness of things long before they reach the upthrusting rock walls where the mountains and the fighting begin.

There is no scale to lay hold on. The largest shells make a smudge no bigger than a midge in a corner of a fold of a swell on the edge of a snowfield's bank. A barracks for two hundred men is a swallow's nest plastered beneath the overhanging eaves, only visible when the light is good – the same light that reveals the glancing spider-web of steel wire strung across the abysses, which is the aerial railway feeding that post. Some of these lines work only by night when travelling cradles that hang from the wires cannot be shrapnelled. Others spin and whisper busily all day, against rifts and chimneys of the rock, with their loads of building material, food, ammunition, and the blessed letter from home, or a still burden of wounded, two at a time, slung down after some fight on the very crest itself. From the wire rope and its cradle, to the mule who carries two hundred pounds, to the five-tonne lorry or the cart, to the rail-head, is the way of it for every ounce of weight that travels up or down this battle-front. Except the big guns. They arrive at their proper place by the same means that Rome was built.

Men explained and re-explained their transport to me, giving weights, sizes, distances, and average allowance per head of troops. Their system is not like ours. It seems to lack our abundance of forms and checks, as well as palaces full of khakied clerks initialling bits of paper in quadruplicate.

'Oh, but we have forms and paper enough,' they protested. 'Any amount of forms. You'll find them in the cities. They don't grow well in the snow here.'

'That sounds reasonable,' I replied, 'but it is the infinite labour imposed on you by your mere surroundings that impresses me most of all. Everything you handle seems to end in a two-hundred-pound package taken up the side of a house, and yet you have heavy artillery on the edge of glaciers. It's a new convention.'

'True. But these are our surroundings, and our people are used to them. They are used to getting load up and down hill; used to handling things and straps and gears and harness and beasts and stones all their lives; besides, we've been at it for two years. That is why the procession moves.'

Yet I came on one ghastly break in it, nevertheless.

There had been a battery with guns, mules, barracks, and stables complete, established on a mountain side, till it had seemed good to the mountain to brush them away as a woman brushes off snow from her skirt. 'Ninety are down below in the valley with the mules and the rest. Those we shall never find. How did it happen? A very little thing starts an avalanche when the snow is ripe for it. Perhaps a rifle-shot. And yet,' he added grimly, 'we must go on and shake all this atmosphere with our guns. Listen!'

There was nothing doing, at the moment, on this front any more than the others – only a hidden piece here or there answering its opponent. Sometimes the discharge sounded like a triumphant whoop across the snows! Then like the fall of trees far off in the thick woods! But it was most awful when it died down to a dumbed beat no louder than the pulse of blood in one's ears after a climb, or that hint which a mountain-slide might give before it chose to move into action on its own.

IV

ONLY A FEW STEPS HIGHER UP

JUNE 16TH 1917

FOR a special job, specialists, but for all jobs, youth above everything! That portion of the Italian frontier where men must mountaineer as well as climb is held with the Alpine regiments. The corps is recruited from the people who inhabit, and know what is in the mind of, the mountains – men used to carry loads along eighteen-inch paths round thousand foot drops. Their talk is the slang of mountains, with a special word for every mood and state of snow, ice, or rock, as elaborately particular as a Zulu's talk when he is describing his cattle. They wear a smash hat adorned with one eagle feather (worn down to an honourable stump, now); the nails upon their boots resemble, and are kept as sharp as the fangs of wolves; their eyes are like our airman's eyes; their walk on their own ground suggests the sea; and a more cheery set of hard-bitten, clean-skinned, steady-eyed young devils I have never yet had the honour to meet.

'What do you do?' I was foolish enough to demand of them from the security of a Mess-room seven thousand feet up among pines and snows. For the moment, the forest cut off the oppression of the mountain view.

'Oh, come and see,' said these joyous children. 'We are working a few steps higher up the road. It is only a few steps.'

They took me by car above the timber-line on the edge of the basin, to the steep foot of a dominant rock wall which I had seen approaching, for hours back, along the road. Twenty or thirty miles away the pillared mass of it had looked no more than implacably hostile – much as Mont Blanc looks from the lake. Coming nearer it had grown steeper, and a wilderness of wrathful crags and fissures had revealed itself. At close range from almost directly below, the thing, one perceived, went up sheer, where it did not bulge outward, like a ship's side at launching. Every monstrous detail of its face, etched by sunshine through utterly clear air, crashed upon the sight at once, overwhelming the mind as a new world might, wearying the eye as a gigantically enlarged photograph does.

It was hidden by a snow tunnel, wide enough for a vehicle and two mules. The tunnel was dingy brown where its roof was thick, and lighted by an unearthly blue glare where it was thin, till it broke into blinding daylight where the May heat had melted out the arch of it. But there was graded gravel underfoot all the way, and swilling gutters carried off the snow-drip on either side. In the open or in the dark, Italy, makes but one kind of road.

'This is our new road', the joyous children explained. 'It isn't quite finished, so if you'll sit on this mule, we'll take you the last few steps, only a few steps higher.'

I looked up again between the towering snowbanks. There were not even wrinkles on the face of the mountain now, but horrible, smooth honey-coloured thumbs and pinnacles, clustered like candle-drippings round the main core of unaffected rock, and the whole framing of it bent towards me.

The road was a gruel of gravel, stones, and working-parties. No one hurried; no one got in his neighbour's way; there were very few orders; but even as the mule hoisted herself up and round the pegged-out turns of it, the road seemed to be drawing itself into shape.

There are little engine-houses at the foot of some of the Swiss bob-runs which, for fifty centimes, used to hoist sportsmen and their bob-sleds up to the top again by funicular. The same arrangement stood on a platform nicked out of rock with the very same smell of raw planks, petrol, and snow, and the same crunch of crampons on slushy ground. But instead of the cog-railway, a steel wire, supported on frail struts and carrying a steel-latticed basket, ran up the face of the rock at an angle which need not be specified. Qua railway, it was nothing – the merest grocery line, they explained – and, indeed, one had seen larger and higher ones in the valleys lower down; but a certain nakedness of rock and snow beneath, and side-way blasts of air out of funnels and rifts that we slid past, made it interesting.

At the terminus, four or five hundred feet overhead (we were more than two thousand feet above the Mess-house in the pines), there was a system – it suggested the marks that old ivy prints on a wall after you peel it off – of legends and paths of slushy trampled snow, connecting the barracks, the cook-house, the Officers' Mess and, I presume, the parade ground of the garrison. If the cook dropped a bucket, he had to go down six hundred feet to retrieve it. If a visitor went too far round a corner to admire the panoramas, he became visible to unartistic Austrians who promptly loosed off a shrapnel. All this eagle's nest of a world in two dimensions boiled with young life and energy, as the planks and girders, the packages of other stuff came up the aerial; and the mountain above leaned outward over it all, hundreds of feet yet to the top.

'Our real work is a little higher up – only a few steps,' they urged.

But I recalled that it was Dante himself who says how bitter it is to climb up and down other people's stairs. Besides, their work was of no interest to any one except the enemy round the corner. It was just the regular routine of these parts. They outlined it for the visitor.

You climb up a fissure of a rock chimney – by shoulder or knee work such as mountaineers understand – and at night for choice, because, by day, the enemy drops stones down the chimney, but then they had to carry machine-guns, and some other things, with them. ('By the way, some of our machine-guns are of French manufacture, so our Machine Gun Corps' souvenir – please take it, we want you to have it – represents the heads of France and Italy side by side.')

And when you emerge from your chimney – which it is best to do in a storm or a gale, since nailed boots on rock make a noise – you find either that you command the enemy's post on the top, in which case you destroy him, or cut him off from supplies by gunning the only goat-path that brings them; or you find the enemy commands you from some unsuspected cornice or knob of rock. Then you go down again – if you can – and try elsewhere. And that is how it is done all along that section of frontier where the ground does not let you do otherwise.

Special work is somewhat different. You select a mountain-top which you have reason to believe is filled with the enemy and all his works. You effect a lodgement there with your teeth and toe-nails; you mine into the solid rock with compressed-air drills for as many hundred yards as you calculate may be necessary. When you have finished, you fill your galleries with nitroglycerine and blow the top off the mountain. Then you occupy the crater with men and machine-guns as fast as you can. Then you secure your dominating position from which you can gain other positions, by the same means.

'But surely you know all about this. You've seen the Castelletto,' someone said.

It stood outside in the sunshine, a rifted bastion crowned with peaks like the roots of molar-teeth. The largest peak had gone. A chasm, a crater and a vast rock slide took its place.

Yes, I had seen the Castelletto, but I was interested to see the men who had blown it up.

'Oh, he did that. That's him.'

A man with the eyes of a poet or musician laughed and nodded. Yes, he owned, he was mixed up in the affair of the Castelletto – had written a report on it, too. They had used thirty-five tons of nitroglycerine for that mine. They had brought it up by hand – in the old days when he was a second lieutenant and men lived in tents, before the wire-rope railways were made – a long time ago.

'And your battalion did it all?'

'No – no: not at all, by any means, but – before we'd finished with the Castelletto we were miners and mechanics and all sorts of things we never expected to be. That is the way of this war.'

'And this mining business still goes on?'

Yes: I might take it that the mining business did go on.

And now would I, please, come and listen to a little music from their band? It lived on the rock ledges – and it would play the Regimental and the Company March; but – one of the joyous children shook his head sadly – 'those Austrians aren't really musical. No ear for music at all.'

Given a rock wall that curves over in a sounding-board behind and above a zealous band, to concentrate the melody, and rock ribs on either side to shoot the tune down a thousand feet on to hard snowfields below, and thunderous echoes from every cranny and cul-de-sac along half a mile of resonant mountain-face, the result, I do assure you, reduces Wagner to a whisper. That they wanted Austria was nothing – she was only just round the corner – but it seemed to me that all Italy must hear them across those gulfs of thin air. They brayed, they neighed, and they roared; the bandsmen's faces puckered with mirth behind the brasses, and the mountains faithfully trumpeted forth their insults all over again.

The Company March did not provoke any applause – I expect the enemy had heard it too often. We embarked on national anthems. The Marsellaise was but a success d'estime, drawing a perfunctory shrapnel or so, but when the band gave them and the whole accusing arch of heaven the Brabanconne the enemy were much moved.

'I told you they had no taste,' said a young faun on a rock shelf; 'still, it shows the swine have a conscience.'

But some folk never know when to stop; besides, it was time for the working-parties to be coming in off the roads. So an announcement was made from high overhead to our unseen audience that the performance was ended and they need not applaud any longer. It was put a little more curtly than this, and it sounded exactly like ears being boxed.

The silence spread with the great shadows of the rock towers across the snow: there was tapping and clinking and an occasional stone-slide far up the mountain side; the aerial railway carried on as usual; the working parties knocked off, and piled tools, and the night shifts began.

The last I saw of the joyous children was a cluster of gnome-like figures a furlong overhead, standing, for there was no visible foothold, on nothing. They separated, and went about their jobs as single dots, moving up or sideways on the face of the rock, till they disappeared into it like ants. Their real work lay 'only a few steps higher up' where the observation-posts, the sentries, the supports and all the rest live on ground compared with which the baboon-tracks round the Mess and the barracks are level pavement. Those rounds must be taken in every weather and light; that is, made at eleven thousand feet, with death for company under each foot, and the width of a foot on each side, at every step of the most uneventful round. Frosty glazed rock where a blunt-nailed boot slips once and no more; mountain blasts round the corner of ledges before the body is braced to them; a knob of rotten shale crumbling beneath the hand; an ankle twisted at the bottom of a ninety-foot rift; a roaring descent of rocks loosened by snow from some corner the sun has undermined through the day – these are a few of the risks they face going from and returning to the coffee and gramophones at the Mess, 'in the ordinary discharge of their duties.'

A turn of the downward road shut them and their world from sight – never to be seen again by my eyes, but the hot youth, the overplus of strength, the happy, unconsidered insolence of it all, the gravity, beautifully maintained over the coffee cups, but relaxed when the band played to the enemy, and the genuine, boyish kindness, will remain with me. But, behind it all, fine as the steel wire ropes, implacable as the mountain, one was conscious of the hardness of their race.

V

THE TRENTINO FRONT
JUNE 20TH 1918

IT does not need an expert to distinguish the notes of the several Italian fronts. One picks them up a long way behind the lines, from the troops in rest or the traffic on the road. Even behind Browning's lovely Asolo where, you will remember, Pippa passed, seventy-six years since, announcing that 'All's right with the world,' one felt the tightening in the air.

The officer, too, explained frankly above his map:

'See where our frontier west of the Dolomites dips south in this 'V'-like spearhead. That's the Trentino. Garibaldi's volunteers were in full possession of it in our War of Independence. Prussia was our ally then against Austria, but Prussia made peace when it suited her – I'm talking of 1864 – and we had to accept the frontier that she and Austria laid down. The Italian frontier is a bad one everywhere – Prussia and Austria took care of that – but the Trentino section is specially bad.' Mist wrapped the plateau we were climbing. The mountains had changed into rounded, almost barrel-shaped heights, steep above dry valleys. The roads were many and new, but the lorries held their pace; the usual old man and young boy were there to see to that. Scotch moors, red uplands, scarred with trenches and punched with shell-holes, a confusion of hills without colour and, in the mist, almost without shape, rose and dropped behind us. They hid the troops in their folds – always awaiting troops – and the trenches multiplied themselves high and low on their sides.

We descended a mountain smashed into rubbish from head to heel, but still preserving the outline, like wrinkles on a forehead, of trenches that had followed its contours. A narrow, shallow ditch (it might have been a water-main) ran vertically up the hill, cutting the faded trenches at right angles.

'That was where our men stood before the Austrians were driven back in their last push - the Asiago push, don't you call it? It took the Austrians ten days to work half-way down from the top of the mountain. Our men drove that trench straight up the hill, as you see. Then they climbed, and the Austrians broke. It's not as bad as it looks, because, in this sort of work, if the enemy uphill misses his footing, he rolls down among your men, but if you stumble, you only slip back among your friends.'

'What did it cost you?' I whispered.

'A good deal. And on that mountain across the gorge – but the mist won't let you see it – our men fought for a week – mostly without water. The Austrians were the first people to

42

lay out a line of twelve-inch shell-holes on a mountain's side to serve as trenches. It's almost a regulation trick on all the fronts now, but it's annoying.'

He told tales of the long, bitter fight when the Austrians thought, till General Cadorna showed them otherwise, they had the plains to the south at their mercy. I should not care to be an Austrian with the Boche behind me and the Exercitus Romanus in front.

It was the quietest of fronts and the least ostentatious of armies. It lived in great towns among forests where we found snow again in dirty, hollow-flanked drifts, that were giving up all the rubbish and refuse that winter had hidden. Labour battalions dealt with the stuff, and there were no smells. Other gangs mended shell-holes with speed; the lorries do not like being checked.

Another township, founded among stones, stood empty except for the cooks and a bored road-mender or two. The population was up the hill digging and blasting; or in wooded park-like hollows of lowland. Battalions slipped like shadows through the mists between the pines. When we reached the edge of everything, there was, as usual, nothing whatever, except uptorn breadths of grass and an 'unhealthy' house – the battered core of what had once been human – with rainwater dripping through the starred ceilings. The view from it included the sight of the Austrian trenches on pale slopes and the noise of Austrian guns – not lazy ones this time, but eager, querulous, almost questioning.

There was no reply from our side. 'If they want to find out

anything, they can come and look,' said the officer.

One speculated how much the men behind those guns would have given for a seat in the car through the next few hours that took us along yet another veiled line of arms. But perhaps by now the Austrians have learned.

The mist thickened around us, and the far shoulders of mountains, and the suddenly-seen masses of men who loomed out of it and were gone. We headed upwards till the mists met the clouds, by a steeper road than any we had used before. It ended in a rock gallery where immense guns, set to a certain point when a certain hour should come, waited in the dark.

'Mind how you walk! It's rather a sharp turn there.'

The gallery came out on a naked space, and a vertical drop of hundreds of feet of striated rock tufted with heath in bloom. At the wall-foot the actual mountain, hardly less steep, began, and, far below that again, flared outward till it became more reasonable slopes, descending in shoulders and knolls to the immense and ancient plains four thousand feet below.

The mists obscured the northern views, but to the southward one traced the courses of broad rivers, the thin shadows of aqueducts, and the piled outlines of city after city whose single past was worth more than the future of all the barbarians clamouring behind the ranges that were pointed out to us through the observatory windows. The officer finished his tales of year-long battles and bombardments among them.

'And that nick in the skyline to the right of that smooth crest under the clouds is a mine we sprung,' said he.

The observation shutter behind its fringe of heather-bells

closed softly. They do everything without noise in this hard and silent land.

THE NEW ITALY

Setting aside the incredible labour of every phase of the Italian war, it is this hardness that impresses one at every turn – from the stripped austerity of General Cadorna's headquarters, which might be a monastery or a laboratory, down to the wayside muleteer, white with dust, but not a bead of sweat on him, working the ladder-like mountain trails behind his animal, or the single sentry lying-out like a panther pressed against a hump of rock, and still as the stone except for his shadowed eyes. There is no pomp, parade, or gallery play anywhere, nor even, as far as can be seen, a desire to turn the best side of things to the light. 'Here,' everybody seems to imply, 'is the work we do. Here are the men and the mechanisms we use. Draw your own conclusions.' No one is hurried or over-pressed, and the 'excitable Latin' of the Boche legend does not appear. One finds, instead, a balanced and elastic system, served by passionate devotion, which saves and spares in the smallest details as wisely and with as broad a view as it drenches the necessary position with the blood of twenty thousand men.

Yet it is not inhuman nor oppressive, nor does it claim to be holy. It works as the Italian, or the knife, works – smoothly and quietly, up to the hilt, maybe. The natural temperateness and open-air existence of the people, their strict training in economy, and their readiness to stake life lightly on personal issues have evolved this system or, maybe, their secular instinct for administration had been reborn under the sword.

When one considers the whole massed scheme of their work one leans to the first opinion; when one looks at the faces of their generals, chiselled out by war to the very cameos of their ancestors under the Roman eagles, one inclines to the second.

Italy, too, has a larger number than most countries of men returned from money-getting in the western republics, who have settled down at home again. (They are called Americanos. They have used the new world, but love the old.) Theirs is a curiously spread influence which, working upon the national quickness of mind and art, makes, I should imagine, for invention and faculty. Add to this the consciousness of the New Italy created by its own immense efforts and necessities – a thing as impossible as dawn to express in words or to miss in the air – and one begins to understand what sort of future is opening for this oldest and youngest among the nations. With thrift, valour, temperance, and an idea, one goes far.

They are fighting now, as all civilisation fights, against the essential devildom of the Boche, which they know better than we do in England, because they were once his ally.

To that end they give, not wasting or sparing, the whole of their endevour. But they are under no illusions as to guarantees of safety necessary after the War, without which their own existence cannot be secured. They fight for these also, because, like the French, they are logical and face facts to the end.

Their difficulties, general and particular, are many. But Italy accepts these burdens and others in just the same spirit as she accepts the cave-riddled plateaux, the mountains, the unstable snows and rocks and the inconceivable toil that they impose upon her arms. They are hard, but she is harder.

Yet, what man can set out to judge anything? In an hotel waiting for a midnight train, an officer was speaking of some of d'Annunzio's poetry that has literally helped to move mountains in this war. He explained an allusion in it by a quotation from Dante. An old porter, waiting for our luggage, dozed crumpled up in a chair by the veranda. As he caught the long swing of the verse, his eyes opened! His chin came out of his shirt-front, till he sat like a little hawk on a perch, attentive to each line, his foot softly following its cadence.